HOW TO
PRAY
the Chaplet of the
DIVINE
MERCY

HOW TO
PRAY
the Chaplet of the
DIVINE
MERCY

Wyatt North
BOOKS THAT INSPIRE

CONTENTS

About Wyatt North...vi

What Is the Chaplet of the Divine Mercy? 1
Who Was St. Faustina? 2
The Revelation of the Chaplet of the Divine Mercy 6
Methods of Praying the Chaplet...8
When to Pray the Chaplet 11

ABOUT WYATT NORTH

STARTING OUT WITH just one writer in 2012, Wyatt North Publishing has expanded to include writers from across the country. Our writers include college professors, theologians, and historians. Wyatt North is a trusted source for Catholic readers looking for inspirational books. Visit WyattNorth.com to sign up for free books and promotions, and to view our catalog.

WHAT IS THE CHAPLET
OF THE DIVINE MERCY?

*T*HE CHAPLET IS rooted in traditional themes of God's mercy, particularly for those burdened in their consciences by sin. It is based on the biblical truth that God is merciful and gracious and that, in turn, having benefitted from God's graces, we must be merciful to others in kind. As such, the Chaplet is appropriate for all Christians to pray, regardless of circumstances. St. Faustina, who, after a vision from Christ, created the Chaplet of the Divine Mercy, recommended the Chaplet especially to those who are particularly vexed by a sinful past or the ongoing struggle against habitual or persistent sin in the present.

The Chaplet of the Divine Mercy is meant to be an extension of what is offered at the Eucharist. Based on Christ's sacrifice, the Chaplet encourages us to live our lives in imitation of Christ's sacrifice by demonstrating acts of mercy to others even as we rest in His mercy ourselves. The Chaplet has often been praised as a particularly powerful act of piety that gives strength to those enduring suffering, plagued by sin, and who are aging and dying.

WHO WAS ST. FAUSTINA?

S AINT MARIA FAUSTINA Kowalska of the Blessed Sacrament was born as Helena Kowalska, the third of ten children to an impoverished but devout family in Głogowiec, a village to the north-west of Łódź in Poland, on August 25, 1905. St. Faustina was beatified by Pope John Paul II on April 18, 1993, and canonized by Pope John Paul II on April 30, 2000.

From a young age, Faustina felt called to the religious life. At age seven, she attended the Exposition of the Blessed Sacrament for her schooling. Afterward, at the age of sixteen, she wished to join a convent, but her parents refused to allow it. Instead, she became a housekeeper and remained at home helping her aging and ailing parents.

Faustina had her first vision of Jesus in 1924. According to Faustina's diaries, while she was attending a dance with her sister, Natalia, an image of the suffering Jesus appeared to her. She immediately went to the Cathedral to pray. By her testimony, during her prayers, Jesus instructed her to depart her hometown and go to Warsaw and join a convent.

Despite her parents' former objections, Faustina returned home and immediately began packing her bags. Upon arrival, the first church she found was Saint James Church. She attended mass there before she even found a place to sleep. During her time in Warsaw, she approached several convents but was refused admittance. There were various reasons why, she was told, that she was unfit for monastic life, ranging from her unkempt appearance to her poor background.

Finally, she found a convent willing to accept her on the condition that, according to the mother superior at the Congregation of the Sisters of Our Lady of Mercy, she could save the money to pay for her own religious habit. Again, Faustina took work as a housekeeper to save her money. On April 30, 1926, she was twenty years old when she received her habit. She assumed, at this time, the name of Sister Marie Faustina of the Blessed Sacrament. She took her vows as a nun in 1928.

As a nun, Faustina played her part serving as a cook and traveled to several convents to serve in this role. In May 1930, at a convent on Plock, Poland, Faustina fell ill and was soon returned to her home convent in Warsaw to rest and recover. It was less than a year later when she had her second "vision" of Jesus.

On February 22, 1931, Jesus presented himself to Faustina in visual form as the "King of Divine Mercy." According to St. Faustina's testimony, he was wearing a white garment adorned with red and pale rays of light emanating from his heart. As he spoke, the Lord directed her to become the apostle and secretary of God's mercy. She was to serve as an exemplar of God's merciful plan for the world—both by humbly receiving God's mercies in her own life and demonstrating His mercy by being merciful to others.

In St. Faustina's diary, she described the vision accordingly:

"In the evening, when I was in my cell, I became aware of the Lord Jesus clothed in a white garment. One hand was raised in blessing; the other was touching the garment at the breast. From the opening of the garment at the breast, there came forth two large rays, one red and the other pale. In silence, I gazed intently at the Lord; my soul was overwhelmed with fear but also with great joy. After a while, Jesus said to me, 'Paint an image according to the pattern you see, with the inscription: Jesus, I trust in You.'"

In the same vision, Jesus also told St. Faustina that the image of Divine Mercy should be "solemnly blessed on the first Sunday after Easter; that Sunday is to be the Feast of Mercy." But this "image," one shown to her the vision, was not one she knew how to produce. She had no training as an artist. Instead, she asked around her convent for help from someone appropriately skilled but found no one suitable to prepare the image. Finally, three years later, in 1934, the first painting of the image—one that Faustina said was precisely the one shown in her vision—was painted by Eugene Kazimierowski.

Not everyone accepted Faustina's claim or directions. In 1932, she prepared to take her final vows in Warsaw, which were said on May 1, 1933. At that point, she became a perpetual sister of Our Lady of Mercy and was immediately thereafter transferred to Vilinius. There, she met Father Michael Spocoko, who had been appointed as confessor for the nuns. During her first confession, she shared her vision and conversation with Jesus with Father Confessor, including what Jesus had told her to do. Father Sopocko, skeptical of her claims, immediately ordered that she be psychiatrically evaluated. This was done not because her confessor believed she was mentally ill or imbalanced but as a measure meant to "test" the spirits to ensure that her vision was genuine and not the product of a cognitive delusion. After Faustina passed the requisite psychological tests, Sopoćko became one of her leading supporters.

It was at Sopoćko's encouragement that Faustina began keeping her diaries—which remain one of the most valuable resources and testimonies to Faustina's experiences to this day. In her diaries, Sopoćko insisted that she record her conversations with Jesus verbatim with as much precision as memory allowed. It was Sopoćko, in fact, who introduced Faustina to Kazimirowski, the artist who eventually painted the first Divine Mercy image.

On Good Friday, April 19, 1935, Jesus appeared to St. Faustina again and told her that he wanted the Divine Mercy image honored publicly. This happened on April 26, 1935, and Father Sopoćko delivered the first sermon on Divine Mercy, which is now a tradition of the appointed feast day. In September of the same year, Faustina wrote that Jesus appeared to her to give her the Chaplet of Divine Mercy—a prayer to be sued to obtain mercy, trust in Christ's mercy, and show His mercy to others.

Encouraged by the reception of the Chaplet, the following year, Faustina took steps to establish a new congregation for Divine Mercy. However, since she was perpetually vowed to her current order, she was sent back to Warsaw. Dejected by this turn of events, Jesus appeared to her again and consoled her, saying, "My Daughter, do whatever is within your power to spread devotion to My Divine Mercy. I will make up for what you lack."

Faustina spent much of the year 1936 ill again and at a sanatorium in Prądnik, Krakow. According to her diary, she spent most of her time there in prayer. Faustina's health, however, continued to decline. In July 1937, the first holy cards with the Divine Mercy image were corrected along with instructions for the Novena of Divine Mercy—a message she again attributed to Jesus as he appeared to her in visions. Her visions intensified as her health continued to fail. On October 5, 1938, Faustina passed away. She was buried two days later at the Basilica of Divine Mercy in Krakow, Poland.

THE REVELATION OF THE CHAPLET OF THE DIVINE MERCY

*O*N SEPTEMBER 13, 1935, in Vilnius, Lithuania, St. Mary Faustina Kowalska recorded a vision in her diary that she had previously received by divine revelation from Jesus Christ. According to St. Faustina, Christ asked her to pray the Chaplet according to the method outlined below and encourage others to do the same. The following words were recorded by St. Faustina regarding the revelation:

"In the evening, when I was in my cell, I saw an Angel, the executor of divine wrath. He was clothed in a dazzling robe, his face gloriously bright, a cloud beneath his feet. From the cloud, bolts of thunder and flashes of lightning were springing into his hands; and from his hand, they were going forth, and only then were they striking the earth. When I saw this sign of divine wrath, which was about to strike the earth, and in particular a certain place, which for good reasons I cannot name, I began to implore the Angel to hold off for a few moments, and the world would do penance. But my plea was a mere nothing in the face of the divine anger. Just then, I saw the Most Holy Trinity. The greatness of Its majesty pierced me deeply, and I did not dare to

repeat my entreaties. At that very moment, I felt in my soul the power of Jesus's grace, which dwells in my soul. When I became conscious of this grace, I was instantly snatched up before the Throne of God. Oh, how great is our Lord and God, and how incomprehensible His holiness! I will make no attempt to describe this greatness because, before long, we shall all see Him as He is. I found myself pleading with God for the world with words heard interiorly.

As I was praying in this manner, I saw the Angel's helplessness: he could not carry out the just punishment, which was rightly due for sins. Never before had I prayed with such inner power as I did then. The words with which I entreated God are these: Eternal Father, I offer You the Body and Blood, Soul and Divinity of Your dearly beloved Son, Our Lord Jesus Christ, for our sins and those of the whole world; for the sake of His sorrowful Passion, have mercy on us.

The next morning, when I entered the chapel, I heard these words interiorly: 'Every time you enter the chapel, immediately recite the prayer I taught you yesterday.' When I had said the prayer, in my soul, I heard these words: 'This prayer will serve to appease My wrath. You will recite it for nine days, on the beads of the Rosary, in the following manner: First of all, you will say one OUR FATHER and HAIL MARY and the I BELIEVE IN GOD. Then on the OUR FATHER beads, you will say the following words: "Eternal Father, I offer You the Body and Blood, Soul and Divinity of Your dearly beloved Son, Our Lord Jesus Christ, in atonement for our sins and those of the whole world." On the HAIL MARY beads, you will say the following words: "For the sake of His sorrowful Passion, have mercy on us and on the whole world." In conclusion, three times you will recite these words: "Holy God, Holy Mighty One, Holy Immortal One, have mercy on us and on the whole world."'"

METHODS OF PRAYING
THE CHAPLET

The Chaplet may be followed using three different methods:

1. *With Traditional Rosary Beads.*
    Even though the Chaplet is about a third of the length of the
    Rosary, with several "decades" (sets of ten) of beads devoted to
    repetition, the Chaplet is most commonly prayed this way. Not
    all of the beads will be used; nonetheless, as many who pray the
    Rosary regularly understand that the use of the Rosary helps
    the person praying the Chaplet focus one's attention on each
    petition, concluding it properly before moving on to the next. It
    can also help ensure that the person praying the Chaplet from
    memory follows it properly, including all the petitions in their
    proper order. As indicated by St. Faustina's revelation above, this
    was the original method for praying the Chaplet.

2. *With Universal Anglican Prayer Beads.*
    Anglican prayer beads (sometimes called the "Anglican Rosary"
    or "Protestant Rosary") consists of only 33 beads compared
    to the 59-bead Catholic Rosary. The 33 beads are meant
    to correspond to each of Christ's 33 years of life before his
    crucifixion. Anglican prayer beads have one invitatory bead just
    above the cross. It is followed by four "weeks" of beads, each

week consisting of seven beads in sequence and separated by a "cruciform" bead.

Despite these differences, these prayer beads serve much the same purpose as a Catholic Rosary. They are meant to help create a focus for contemplative prayer. The Chaplet can be modified to be said according to Universal Anglican Prayer Beads. Instructions for doing this will be included in a separate section below dedicated to this purpose.

3. *Following the Petitions Using One's Fingers.*
Since the Chaplet is divided into roughly ten parts, it is convenient that one can pray it according to each of one's fingers. The primary benefit of this method is that anyone can do it even if he or she does not possess a Rosary or prayer beads, or if one is moved to pray the Chaplet at a moment when one does not have his or her Rosary or beads in hand. The beauty of this method is that no matter where one is or how spontaneous the desire to pray the Chaplet might be, one can still pray the Chaplet without the aid of anything but one's own body.

Any of these methods can be recommended as equally beneficial ways of praying through the Chaplet. The choice of which method is, in part, a reflection of one's background (e.g., Catholics will naturally use a Rosary; Anglicans will likely gravitate toward the use of Universal Anglican Prayer Beads; and anyone might choose, in the absence of either of the above, to use one's ten fingers). Ultimately, however, the method employed is mostly a matter of personal choice. Circumstances may also dictate the choice (e.g., if one does not have his or her Rosary/ beads when one begins the Chaplet).

Any Christian can pray the Chaplet using any of the above methods. While the prayers do not change, the guides below can be followed based on any of the three above choices depending on the method. For simplicity's sake and to ensure that one is not hung up on various competing instructions in the guide, the three methods will be handled separately. Choose the method you would like to follow and then navigate to your preference's corresponding section.

WHEN TO PRAY
THE CHAPLET

*T*HE DIVINE MERCY Chaplet can be prayed at any time. It can be particularly helpful to pray prior to engaging in an act of mercy, such as offering one's service to the poor or hungry. It can be prayed as an extension of the Eucharist, following the reception of the Sacrament, as an impetus to allow Jesus's mercies to flow through us in our daily lives. Finally, it can be used in conjunction with confession as a reminder of God's mercies over our sin.

In addition to these occasions, Jesus also encourages us, through St. Faustina, to pray it at two specific times:

At 3 p.m. each afternoon as Jesus invites us to recall His love for us in His death on the Cross. Jesus said to Faustina: "At three o'clock, implore My mercy, especially for sinners; and, if only for a brief moment, immerse yourself in My Passion, particularly in My abandonment at the moment of agony. This is the hour of great mercy. In this hour, I will refuse nothing to the soul that makes a request of Me in virtue of My Passion."

As a novena (a series of prayers meant to be said over nine consecutive days) before the Feast of Divine Mercy, which is the Sunday after Easter. Jesus said to Faustina: "I desire that during these nine days you bring souls to the fountain of My mercy, that they may draw therefrom strength and refreshment and whatever grace they have need of in the hardships of life, and especially at the hour of death."

Guide: How to Pray the Chaplet (The Rosary Method)

Step 1 — Using a regular set of Rosary beads, you begin at the cross by doing the sign of the cross.

> An optional opening prayer can be recited at this point: *You expired, Jesus, but the source of life gushed forth for souls, and the ocean of mercy opened up for the whole world. O Fount of Life, unfathomable Divine Mercy, envelop the whole world and empty Yourself out upon us. (Repeat three times.) O Blood and Water, which gushed forth from the Heart of Jesus as a fountain of Mercy for us, I trust in You!*

Step 2 — On the three beads of the Rosary, pray the Our Father, the Hail Mary, and the Apostles Creed:

Our Father:
Our Father, Who art in heaven, hallowed be Thy name;
Thy kingdom come; Thy will be done on earth as it is in heaven.
Give us this day our daily bread;
and forgive us our trespasses as we forgive those who trespass against us;
and lead us not into temptation, but deliver us from evil, Amen

The Hail Mary:
Hail Mary, full of grace. The Lord is with thee.
Blessed art thou amongst women and blessed is the fruit of thy womb, Jesus.
Holy Mary, Mother of God, pray for us sinners,
now and at the hour of our death, Amen.

The Apostles Creed:
I believe in God, the Father almighty, creator of heaven and earth,
and in Jesus Christ, his only Son, our Lord, who was conceived by the Holy Spirit,
born of the Virgin Mary, suffered under Pontius Pilate,
was crucified, died, and was buried; he descended into hell;
on the third day, he rose again from the dead;
he ascended into heaven, and is seated at the right hand of God the Father almighty;
from there he will come to judge the living and the dead.
I believe in the Holy Spirit, the holy Catholic Church,
and the communion of saints, the forgiveness of sins,
the resurrection of the body, and life everlasting. Amen

Step 3 — You begin each decade with the Our Father beads by praying this prayer: *Eternal Father, I offer You the Body and Blood, Soul and Divinity of Your dearly beloved Son, Our Lord Jesus Christ, in atonement for our sins and those of the whole world.*

Step 4 — Complete the decade on the ten Hail Mary beads by praying this prayer:

> *For the sake of His sorrowful Passion, have mercy on us and on the whole world.*

Repeat Steps 3 and 4 for each decade on the Rosary beads

Step 5 — Once you have prayed all five decades, you finish the Chaplet by praying the following prayer three times: *Holy God, Holy Mighty One, Holy Immortal One, have mercy on us and on the whole world.*

You may conclude with the following (optional) closing prayer: *Eternal God, in whom mercy is endless and the treasury of compassion inexhaustible, look kindly upon us, and increase Your mercy in us, that in difficult* moments, we might not despair nor become despondent, but with great confidence, submit ourselves to Your holy will, which is Love and Mercy itself. Amen.

Guide: How to Pray the Chaplet (Anglican Prayer Beads)

Step 1 — Using a set of Universal Anglican Prayer Beads, you begin at the cross by doing the sign of the cross.

> An optional opening prayer can be recited at this point: *You expired, Jesus, but the source of life gushed forth for souls, and the ocean of mercy opened up for the whole world. O Fount of Life, unfathomable Divine Mercy, envelop the whole world and empty Yourself out upon us. (Repeat three times.) O Blood and Water, which gushed forth from the Heart of Jesus as a fountain of Mercy for us, I trust in You!*

Step 2 — On the single invitatory bead above the cross, speak the Our Father, the Hail Mary, and the Apostles Creed:
Our Father:
Our Father, Who art in heaven, hallowed be Thy name;
Thy kingdom come; Thy will be done on earth as it is in heaven.
Give us this day our daily bread;
and forgive us our trespasses as we forgive those who trespass against us;
and lead us not into temptation, but deliver us from evil, Amen

The Hail Mary:
Hail Mary, full of grace. The Lord is with thee.
Blessed art thou amongst women and blessed is the fruit of thy womb, Jesus.
Holy Mary, Mother of God, pray for us sinners,
now and at the hour of our death, Amen.

The Apostles Creed:
I believe in God, the Father almighty, creator of heaven and earth,
and in Jesus Christ, his only Son, our Lord, who was conceived by the Holy Spirit,
born of the Virgin Mary, suffered under Pontius Pilate,
was crucified, died, and was buried; he descended into hell;
on the third day, he rose again from the dead;
he ascended into heaven, and is seated at the right hand of God the Father almighty;
from there he will come to judge the living and the dead.
I believe in the Holy Spirit, the holy Catholic Church,
and the communion of saints, the forgiveness of sins,
the resurrection of the body, and life everlasting. Amen

Step 3 — You begin each "week" with the "cruciform" beads by praying this prayer: *Eternal Father, I offer You the Body and Blood, Soul, and Divinity of Your dearly beloved Son, Our Lord Jesus Christ, in atonement for our sins and those of the whole world.*

Step 4 — Complete the week on the seven successive beads by praying this prayer:
> *For the sake of His sorrowful Passion, have mercy on us and on the whole world.*

Repeat Steps 3 and 4 for each cruciform bead and set of weeks.

Step 5 — Once you have prayed all four weeks, you finish the Chaplet by praying the following prayer while once again clinging to the cross: *Holy God, Holy Mighty One, Holy Immortal One, have mercy on us and on the whole world.* (Repeat this prayer three times.)

You may conclude with the following (optional) closing prayer: *Eternal God, in whom mercy is endless and the treasury of compassion inexhaustible, look kindly upon us, and increase*

Your mercy in us, that in difficult moments, we might not despair nor become despondent, but with great confidence, submit ourselves to Your holy will, which is Love and Mercy itself. Amen.

Guide: How to Pray the Chaplet (Using Ten Fingers)

Step 1 — You begin at the cross by doing the sign of the cross.

An optional opening prayer can be recited at this point: *You expired, Jesus, but the source of life gushed forth for souls, and the ocean of mercy opened up for the whole world. O Fount of Life, unfathomable Divine Mercy, envelop the whole world and empty Yourself out upon us. (Repeat three times.) O Blood and Water, which gushed forth from the Heart of Jesus as a fountain of Mercy for us, I trust in You!*

Step 2 – Folding one's hands, so they are clasped in the shape of a cross, pray the Our Father, the Hail Mary, and the Apostles Creed:
Our Father:
Our Father, Who art in heaven, hallowed be Thy name;
Thy kingdom come; Thy will be done on earth as it is in heaven.
Give us this day our daily bread;
and forgive us our trespasses as we forgive those who trespass against us;
and lead us not into temptation, but deliver us from evil, Amen

The Hail Mary:
Hail Mary, full of grace. The Lord is with thee.
Blessed art thou amongst women and blessed is the fruit of thy womb, Jesus.
Holy Mary, Mother of God, pray for us sinners,
now and at the hour of our death, Amen.

The Apostles Creed:
I believe in God, the Father almighty, creator of heaven and earth,
and in Jesus Christ, his only Son, our Lord, who was conceived by the Holy Spirit,
born of the Virgin Mary, suffered under Pontius Pilate,
was crucified, died, and was buried; he descended into hell;
on the third day, he rose again from the dead;
he ascended into heaven, and is seated at the right hand of God the Father almighty;
from there he will come to judge the living and the dead.
I believe in the Holy Spirit, the holy Catholic Church,
and the communion of saints, the forgiveness of sins,
the resurrection of the body, and life everlasting. Amen

Step 3 — You begin each round by praying this prayer: *Eternal Father, I offer You the Body and Blood, Soul and Divinity of Your dearly beloved Son, Our Lord Jesus Christ, in atonement for our sins and those of the whole world.*

Step 4 — Using each of your ten fingers as a guide, pray this prayer ten times:
For the sake of His sorrowful Passion, have mercy on us and on the whole world.

Repeat Steps 3 and 4 four additional times (corresponding with a total of five decades on a traditional Rosary).

Step 5 — You finish the Chaplet by once again folding one's hands, so they are clasped in the shape of the cross, and praying the following prayer three times: *Holy God, Holy Mighty One, Holy Immortal One, have mercy on us and on the whole world.*

You may conclude with the following (optional) closing prayer: *Eternal God, in whom mercy is endless and the treasury of compassion inexhaustible, look kindly upon us and increase Your mercy in us so that in difficult moments, we might not despair nor become despondent, but with great confidence, submit ourselves to Your holy will, which is Love and Mercy itself. Amen.*

CPSIA information can be obtained
at www.ICGtesting.com
Printed in the USA
BVHW051325110123
656088BV00020B/209